Angels

Every Day Thoughts

new seasons®

To:

_____

From:

_____

Karla Dornacher

Artwork © Karla Dornacher
Licensed by J. Countryman
Agent Art Impressions, Inc.

Original inspirations written by Margaret Anne Huffman, Lynn James, Marie D. Jones,
Carol Smith, Anna Trimiew, Lynda Twardowski, Natalie Walker Whitlock, and Gary Wilde

January 1

Angels are the guardians of our hearts
and the keepers of our dreams.

Notes

_____

_____

_____

_____

_____

_____

_____

_____

_____

January 2

Take time for angels and
angels will take time for you.

Anniversary Gifts

	Traditional	Modern		Traditional	Modern
First	Paper	Clock	Twentieth	China	Platinum
Second	Cotton	China	Twenty-fifth	Silver	Silver
Third	Leather	Crystal & Glass	Thirtieth	Pearls	Diamond jewelry
Fourth	Fruit & Flowers	Appliances	Thirty-fifth	Coral	Jade
Fifth	Woodenware	Silverware	Fortieth	Ruby	Ruby
Sixth	Candy & Iron	Woodenware	Forty-fifth	Sapphire	Sapphire
Seventh	Wood & Copper	Desk set	Fiftieth	Gold	Gold
Eighth	Bronze & Pottery	Linen & Lace	Fifty-fifth	Emeralds	Emeralds
Ninth	Pottery & Willow	Leather goods	Sixtieth	Diamonds	Diamonds
Tenth	Tin & Aluminum	Diamond jewelry	Sixty-fifth	Blue sapphire	Blue sapphire
Fifteenth	Crystal	Watch	Seventieth	Platinum	Platinum

January 3

Angels reflect the
magnificence of heaven,
the spectacular home
that God has prepared for
all those who belong to him.

December

Birthdays and Anniversaries

_____   _____

_____   _____

_____   _____

_____   _____

_____   _____

_____   _____

_____   _____

Birthstone: Turquoise
Flower: Poinsettia

The road that leads
us home is winding,
but our angels are kind and
let us go as slowly as
we need in order to
complete the journey.

November
Birthdays and Anniversaries

_____   _____

_____   _____

_____   _____

_____   _____

_____   _____

_____   _____

_____   _____

Birthstone: Topaz
Flower: Chrysanthemum

January 5

When you tickle a
baby, listen carefully!
You will hear angels
giggling and cherubs
cooing with joy.

October
Birthdays and Anniversaries

_____   _____

_____   _____

_____   _____

_____   _____

_____   _____

_____   _____

_____   _____

Birthstone: Opal
Flower: Dahlia

January 6

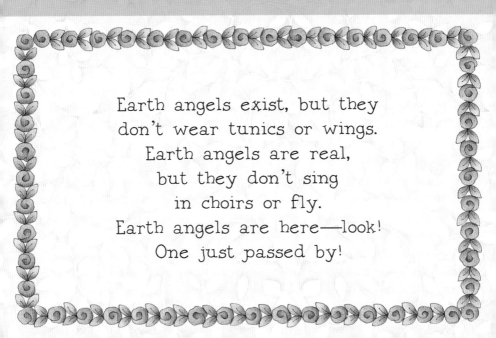

Earth angels exist, but they
don't wear tunics or wings.
Earth angels are real,
but they don't sing
in choirs or fly.
Earth angels are here—look!
One just passed by!

September

Birthdays and Anniversaries

_____   _____

_____   _____

_____   _____

_____   _____

_____   _____

_____   _____

_____   _____

Birthstone: Sapphire

Flower: Aster

January 7

Call on me in
the day of trouble;
I will deliver you,
and you shall glorify me.

~Psalm 50:15

August
Birthdays and Anniversaries

_____   _____

_____   _____

_____   _____

_____   _____

_____   _____

_____   _____

_____   _____

Birthstone: Peridot
Flower: Gladiolus

January 8

God, please allow me to
feel your loving presence
in my worktime,
in my playtime,
in all my time.

July
Birthdays and Anniversaries

1st Zime,
3 Neil,
10, Mum 11 me, 12 Jesse
14 Ezanya, 16 Yvonne

Birthstone: Ruby
Flower: Sweet Pea

January 9

A surgeon's hand, a friend's note,
and a mentor's pat on the back are
all angels in the guise of the ordinary—
carrying us like a thousand lifting wings.

June
Birthdays and Anniversaries

_____   _____

_____   _____

_____   _____

_____   _____

_____   _____

_____   _____

_____   _____

Birthstone: Pearl
Flower: Rose

January 10

Have you ever wished
you could be an angel?
Just help someone in need
and never tell a soul about it.

May
Birthdays and Anniversaries

_____   _____

_____   _____

_____   _____

_____   _____

_____   _____

_____   _____

_____   _____

Birthstone: Emerald
Flower: Lily of the Valley

January 11

He will command
his angels concerning
you, and on their hands
they will bear you up.

~Matthew 4:6

April
Birthdays and Anniversaries

_____   _____

_____   _____

_____   _____

_____   _____

_____   _____

_____   _____

_____   _____

Birthstone: Diamond
Flower: Daisy or Lily

January 12

He will cover you with his
pinions, and under his wings
you will find refuge; his
faithfulness is a shield
and a buckler.

~Psalm 91:4

March
Birthdays and Anniversaries

_____   _____

_____   _____

_____   _____

_____   _____

_____   _____

_____   _____

_____   _____

Birthstone: Aquamarine

Flower: Violet

January 13

Help me to live
well in the
present, and help
me to endure well
to the end so that
I may live in the
presence of angels.

february
Birthdays and Anniversaries

_____   _____

_____   _____

_____   _____

_____   _____

_____   _____

_____   _____

_____   _____

Birthstone: Amethyst
Flower: Primrose

January 14

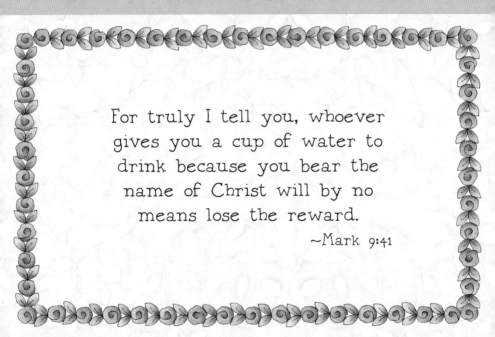

For truly I tell you, whoever gives you a cup of water to drink because you bear the name of Christ will by no means lose the reward.

~Mark 9:41

January

Birthdays and Anniversaries

_____   _____
_____   _____
_____   _____
_____   _____
_____   _____
_____   _____
_____   _____

Birthstone: Garnet
Flower: Carnation

January 15

Hope is that thing
with feathers,
That perches in the soul,
And sings the tune
without words,
And never stops at all.
~Emily Dickinson

December 31

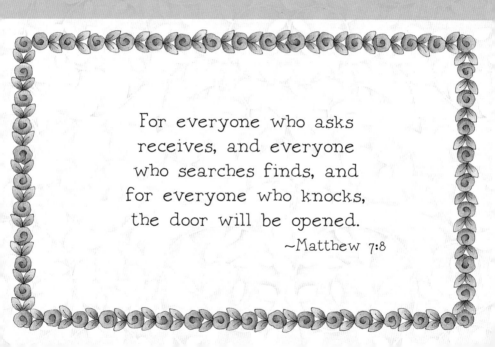

For everyone who asks
receives, and everyone
who searches finds, and
for everyone who knocks,
the door will be opened.

~Matthew 7:8

January 16

Hospitality brings strangers
in, welcomes them as new
friends, then stokes the warming
hearth where all can gather.

December 30

Just as the angels guided
the Wise Men to Christ, so,
too, will angels guide us to
our divine destiny, if we
but have the courage to follow.

January 17

A sweet friend's
voice on a lonely night
is like an angel's song.

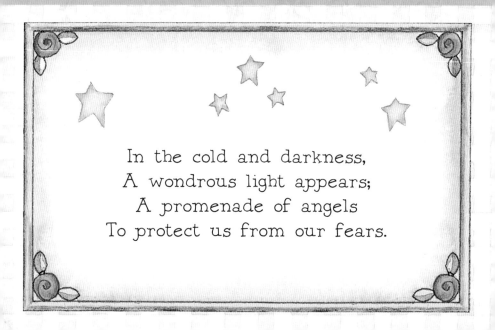

In the cold and darkness,
A wondrous light appears;
A promenade of angels
To protect us from our fears.

January 18

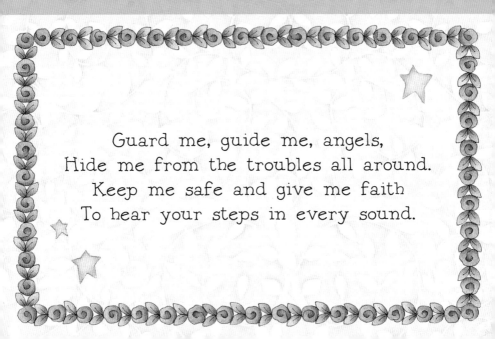

Guard me, guide me, angels,
Hide me from the troubles all around.
Keep me safe and give me faith
To hear your steps in every sound.

December 28

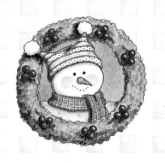

No evil will overcome
you when you walk
with your guardian angel.

January 19

Sing praise!

To hear the
chorus of angels,
listen with
your heart.

December 27

On the day Christ was born,
a choir of angels sang in sweet
harmony as bells of peace pealed
with joy throughout the land.

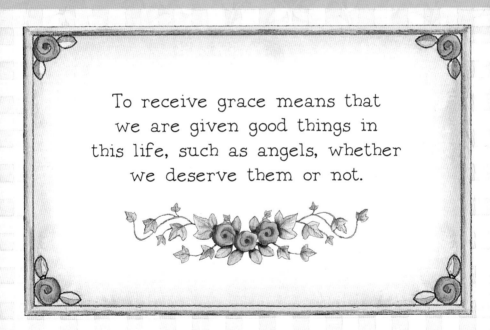

To receive grace means that
we are given good things in
this life, such as angels, whether
we deserve them or not.

December 26

And he said to them,
"Go into all the world and proclaim
the good news to the whole creation."

~Mark 16:15

January 21

Humans are at their best when they are in the company of angels.

But the angel said to them,
"Do not be afraid; for see—I am
bringing you good news of great joy
for all the people: to you is born
this day in the city of David a
Savior, who is the Messiah, the Lord."

~Luke 2:10–11

January 22

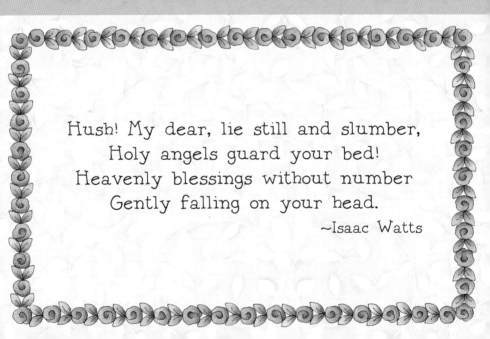

Hush! My dear, lie still and slumber,
Holy angels guard your bed!
Heavenly blessings without number
Gently falling on your head.

~Isaac Watts

Don't resent people's faults and flaws. If we didn't have them, we wouldn't need angels.

January 23

Heed the lesson
of the Lord; only the
faithful shall rise.

December 23

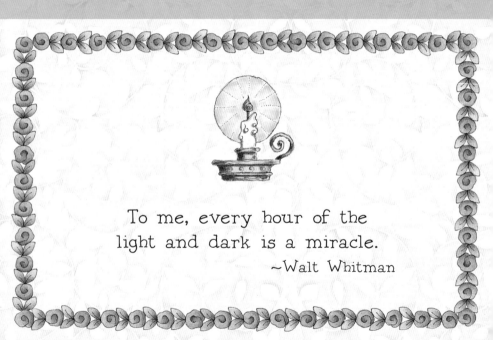

To me, every hour of the
light and dark is a miracle.

~Walt Whitman

January 24

Be filled with the Spirit,
as you sing psalms and hymns
and spiritual songs among
yourselves, singing and making
melody to the Lord in your hearts.

~Ephesians 5:18–19

December 22

Sing praise!

Today I rejoiced in the beauty of life
and love, and I danced with the angels.

January 25

Greet one another with a holy kiss.

~2 Corinthians 13:12

December 21

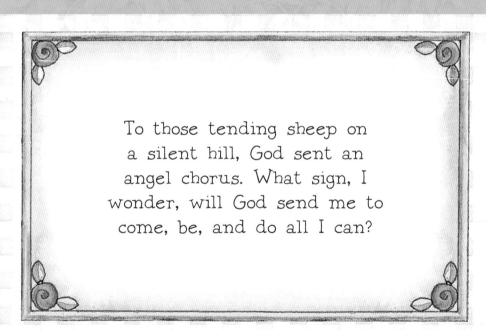

To those tending sheep on a silent hill, God sent an angel chorus. What sign, I wonder, will God send me to come, be, and do all I can?

January 26

I have felt the presence
of my guardian angel in
times of duress like a warm,
comforting breath upon my
face in a cold winter storm.

Whoever shall know
God shall know
his angels.

January 27

I have spread my dreams
under your feet.
Tread softly because you
tread on my dreams.
~William Butler Yeats

December 19

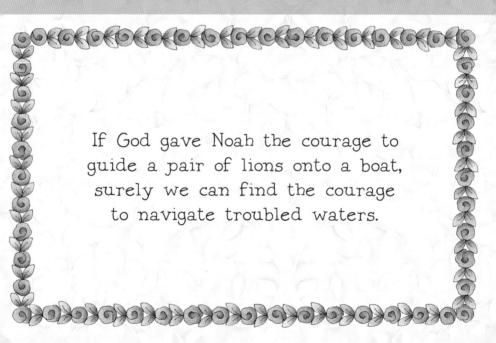

If God gave Noah the courage to guide a pair of lions onto a boat, surely we can find the courage to navigate troubled waters.

January 28

I know that sharing
my own goodness is the
best way to share the Lord.

December 18

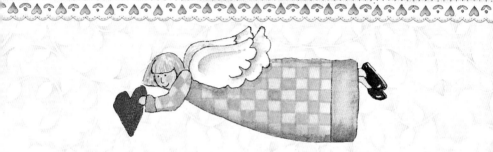

Often we don't know someone is an angel
until they've touched our lives and moved on.

January 29

I will give them one heart,
and put a new spirit within them.

~Ezekiel 11:19

December 17

If you want to know what you're truly capable of, follow God's example.

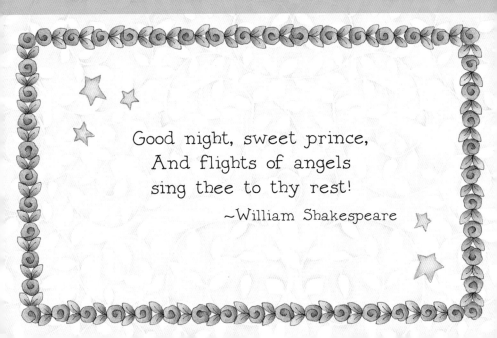

Good night, sweet prince,
And flights of angels
sing thee to thy rest!

~William Shakespeare

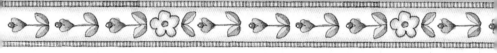

Hunger only for what
nourishes your soul.

Of bread and wine,
I taste only faith.

December 15

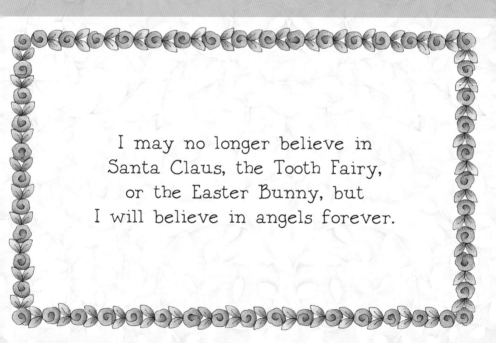

I may no longer believe in
Santa Claus, the Tooth Fairy,
or the Easter Bunny, but
I will believe in angels forever.

Maybe angels don't have wings,
And maybe they don't fly,
But we believe they do exist
Somewhere up on high.

December 14

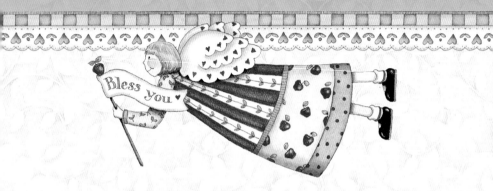

Bless you ♥

Tread in the paths of angels, and
your steps will always be light.

February 2

More things are wrought
by prayer than this
world dreams of.
~Alfred, Lord Tennyson

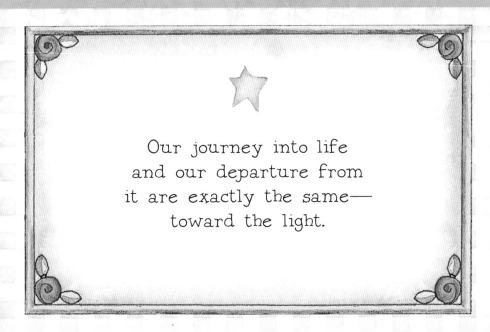

Our journey into life
and our departure from
it are exactly the same—
toward the light.

February 3

May the whispers of
angels guide you through
your darkest hour.

December 12

Whatever my question,
prayer is my answer.

February 4

My prayers for you always
include an angel, because
that's what you are to me.

December 11

To feel the fullness of
our faith, sometimes we
must know the feeling
of emptiness for awhile.

February 5

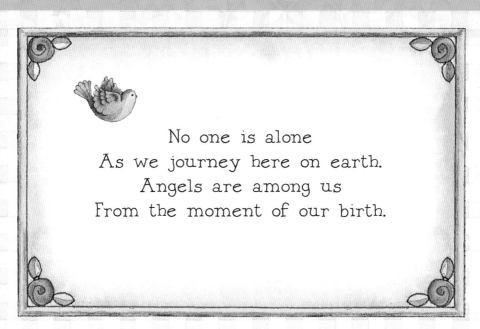

No one is alone
As we journey here on earth.
Angels are among us
From the moment of our birth.

December 10

When you lift someone's
spirit, you can't help
but lift your own.

February 6

How many angels are there?
One—who transforms our life—is plenty.

~Traditional saying

Angels follow your
steps as clearly as
if you are walking
on newly fallen snow.

February 7

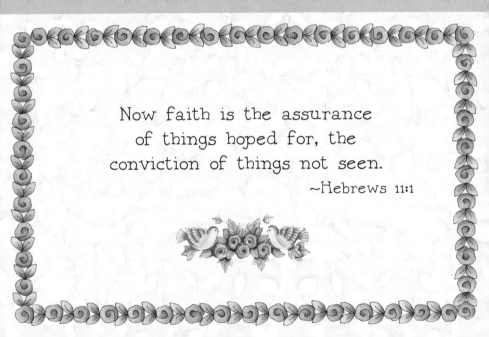

Now faith is the assurance
of things hoped for, the
conviction of things not seen.

~Hebrews 11:1

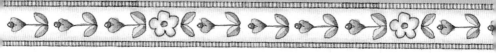

When your wings have been clipped, do as the angels do—hang on to another until you can fly again.

February 8

Now who will harm
you if you are eager
to do what is good?

~1 Peter 3:13

December 7

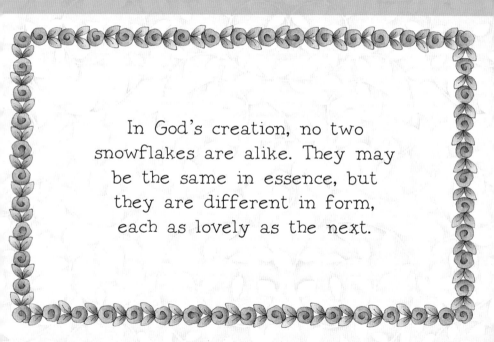

In God's creation, no two
snowflakes are alike. They may
be the same in essence, but
they are different in form,
each as lovely as the next.

February 9

Coincidences are really
angels working behind the
scenes making miracles and
magic out of everyday occurrences.

December 6

Be brave even if
you're not. Only God
knows you are pretending.

February 10

Angels don't have to speak to be heard, be visible to be seen, or be present to be felt. Believe in angels, and they will always be near.

December 5

For once you were darkness,
but now in the Lord you are light.
Live as children of light—for the
fruit of the light is found in all
that is good and right and true.

~Ephesians 5:8-9

February 11

To hope is to fly.
To fly is to dream.
To dream is to believe.
To believe is to do.
To do is to give hope.
To give hope is to
fight the fight of angels.

December 4

We cannot let our angels go; we do not see that they go out that archangels may come in.

~Ralph Waldo Emerson

February 12

Once you find
your angel,
never let her go.

December 3

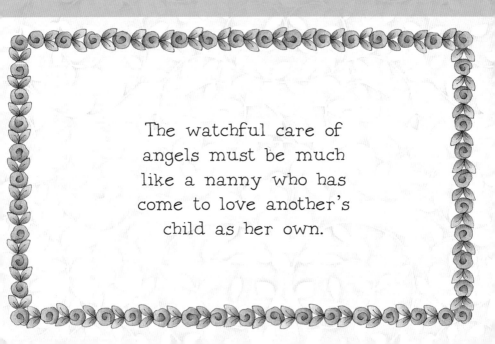

The watchful care of
angels must be much
like a nanny who has
come to love another's
child as her own.

February 13

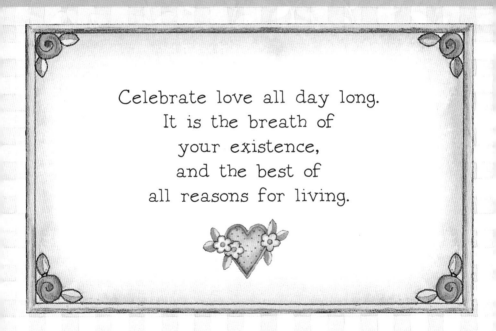

Celebrate love all day long.
It is the breath of
your existence,
and the best of
all reasons for living.

December 2

In my opinion, the Divine is revealed
to all men once at least in their lives.

~Marie Corelli

February 14

Angels breathlessly
wait for us
to choose to love.

December 1

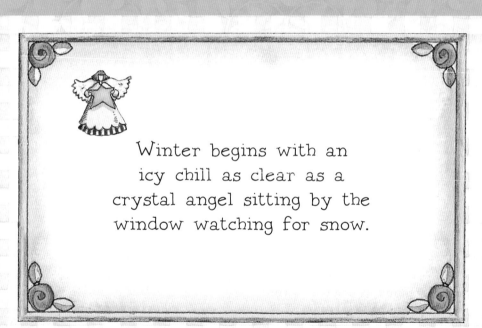

Winter begins with an
icy chill as clear as a
crystal angel sitting by the
window watching for snow.

February 15

Have faith in angels, and
you always have a friend
to talk to, confide in,
and trust until the end.

Spiritual teaching must always be by symbols.

~Mary Baker Eddy

February 16

Forget-Me-Not

Let your
goodness grow.

November 29

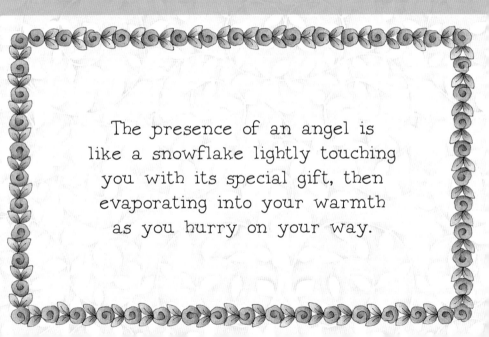

The presence of an angel is
like a snowflake lightly touching
you with its special gift, then
evaporating into your warmth
as you hurry on your way.

February 17

Amid the winds and fires
of my day, may I pause to
hear your stillness speak.

When we are filled with amazement,
we worship like angels.

February 18

One in human form touched
me and strengthened me.

~Daniel 10:18

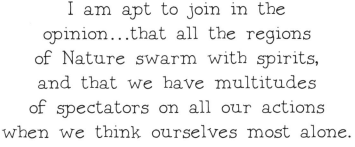

I am apt to join in the
opinion...that all the regions
of Nature swarm with spirits,
and that we have multitudes
of spectators on all our actions
when we think ourselves most alone.

~Joseph Addison

February 19

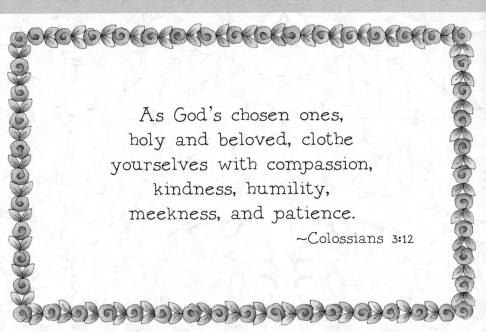

As God's chosen ones,
holy and beloved, clothe
yourselves with compassion,
kindness, humility,
meekness, and patience.

~Colossians 3:12

Millions of spiritual
creatures walk the earth
Unseen, both when we wake,
and when we sleep.

~John Milton

February 20

By this we know that
we abide in him and
he in us, because he has
given us of his Spirit.

~1 John 4:13

Little children lay in snow,
Arms spread wide in winter's glow,
Looking up with laughing eyes,
Making angels just their size.

February 21

Be merciful to me, O God,
be merciful to me, for in
you my soul takes refuge;
in the shadow of your wings
I will take refuge, until the
destroying storms pass by.

~Psalm 57:1

November 24

Angels speak to all
of us; some people
are just listening more
closely than others.

February 22

Powerful warriors
of mercy and love
Pray for us, angels,
Pray for our souls.

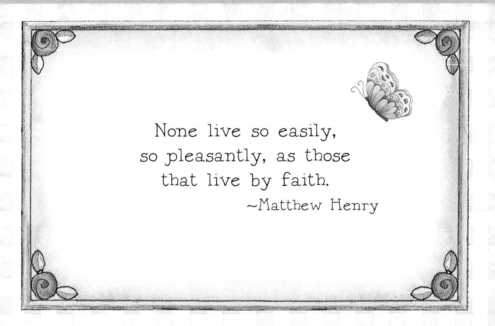

None live so easily,
so pleasantly, as those
that live by faith.

~Matthew Henry

February 23

As you travel life's
winding road
Angels light the way
and share the load.

November 22

Beautiful spirit,
with thy hair of
light and dazzling
eyes of glory!
~Lord George Gordon Byron

February 24

Only through
the lens of
faith can
angels be seen.

November 21

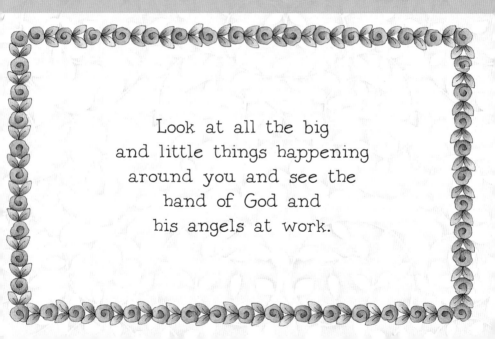

Look at all the big
and little things happening
around you and see the
hand of God and
his angels at work.

February 25

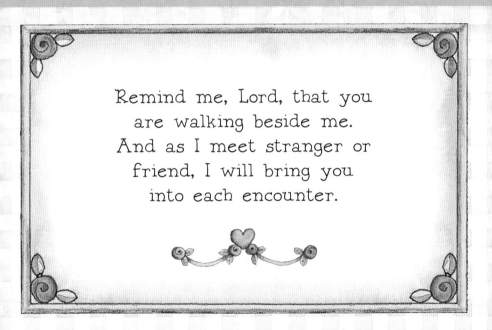

Remind me, Lord, that you
are walking beside me.
And as I meet stranger or
friend, I will bring you
into each encounter.

November 20

Hope steadies the faltering soul.

February 26

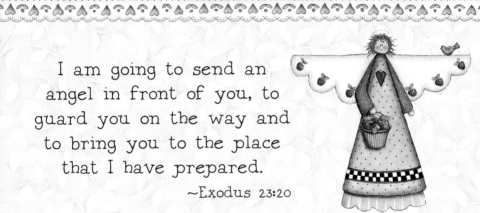

I am going to send an angel in front of you, to guard you on the way and to bring you to the place that I have prepared.

~Exodus 23:20

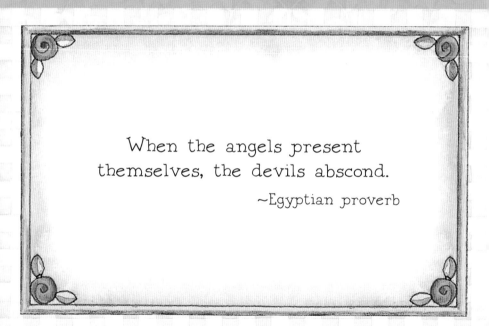

When the angels present
themselves, the devils abscond.

~Egyptian proverb

Sharing daily miracles
with loved ones makes
an ordinary celebration
extraordinary.

November 18

Those who care
for others are
angels on earth.

February 28

Each new day is a
gift from God and
another opportunity
to act like an angel.

November 17

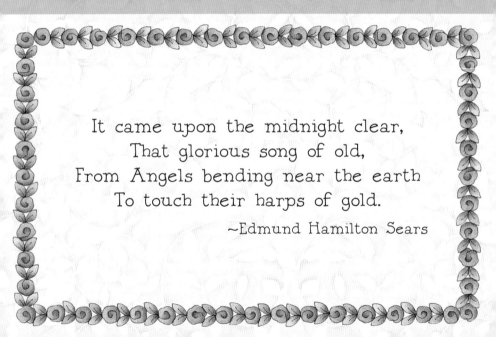

It came upon the midnight clear,
That glorious song of old,
From Angels bending near the earth
To touch their harps of gold.

~Edmund Hamilton Sears

February 29

Believe, give, love, hope—
do these things always.

November 16

Look for the silver lining around
any dark cloud, and you will see
a circle of angels reflecting rays
of hope and circles of joy.

March 1

For where two or three are gathered in my name, I am there among them.

~Matthew 18:20

November 15

I face each day with certainty
And sleep without fear,
For I know the Lord in heaven
Has an angel standing near.

March 2

Angels have appeared
throughout humankind's existence.
They have led the way of kings
and witnessed miracles.
They have protected humanity
and run errands for God.

Angels carry
messages from
heaven to earth.

March 3

Soar with the joy of an
angel into the heart of God,
knowing that God provides,
watches over, and
delights in your flight.

November 13

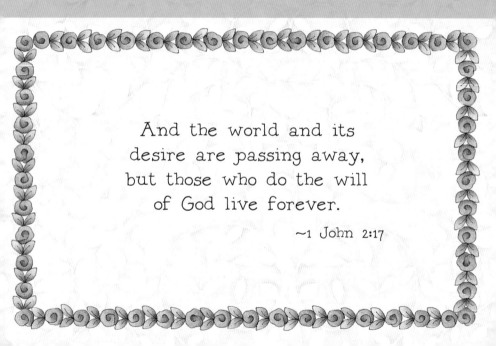

And the world and its
desire are passing away,
but those who do the will
of God live forever.

~1 John 2:17

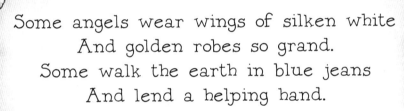

Some angels wear wings of silken white
And golden robes so grand.
Some walk the earth in blue jeans
And lend a helping hand.

November 12

Sing praise!

Angels want nothing from you
but everything for you.

March 5

But the angel who had come
and talked with me held me
and strengthened me
and set me on my feet.

~2 Esdras 5:15

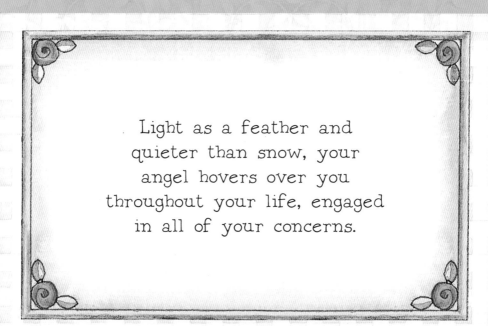

Light as a feather and
quieter than snow, your
angel hovers over you
throughout your life, engaged
in all of your concerns.

March 6

I have heard the bells, seen
the stars, felt the divine.
How could I not believe in angels?

To be without
wings doesn't mean
we can't don a
halo now and then.

I don't need to hear
the whisper of angels.
When I see a flower
flutter in the breeze,
I know they are near.

God may not always
grant us happiness, but
he always grants us hope.

I have often prayed for
an angel, and my angels
have always prayed for me.

November 8

You cannot harm yourself or someone
you love without harming God.

March 9

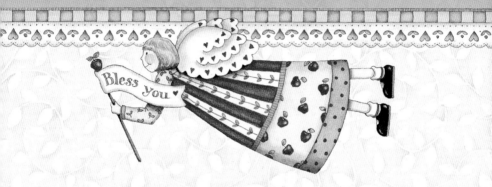

In our darkest days,
angels are the light of God.

We are most like angels
when we stand ready to
serve the good inside of us.

March 10

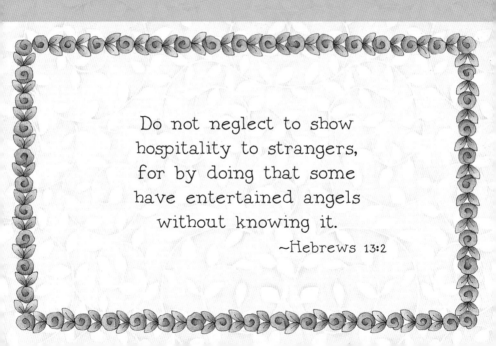

Do not neglect to show
hospitality to strangers,
for by doing that some
have entertained angels
without knowing it.

~Hebrews 13:2

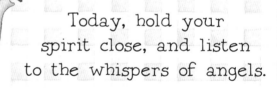

Today, hold your
spirit close, and listen
to the whispers of angels.

March 11

When the road of life
makes you weary
of walking, remember
your wings.

November 5

Let an angel run interference,
and you will find yourself
succeeding every time.

March 12

Do not be conformed to this world,
but be transformed by the renewing
of your minds, so that you may
discern what is the will of God—what
is good and acceptable and perfect.

~Romans 12:2

November 4

Angels do not change your mind; they
wait patiently until you do it yourself.

March 13

Dear God, please show me
how to embrace the joy of angels.

November 3

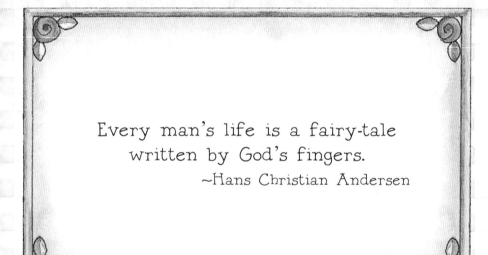

Every man's life is a fairy-tale
written by God's fingers.
~Hans Christian Andersen

March 14

Behind every great human
stands an angel cheering
and urging, guiding and
encouraging, loving and leading.

However fast we move, the pace is never so quick that God cannot meet us there.

March 15

Every raindrop that falls is
accompanied by an Angel.

~Mohammed

Angels rejoice, worship,
and love. They probably
whoop and holler, as well.
For now, we can only
imagine the excitement
in their hometown.

Angels are not only above us;
they are also within us.

October 31

Among my blessings,
I count innumerable angels.

March 17

When we live by God's word, we are all angels.

Sing praise!

October 30

And now faith, hope, and
love abide, these three; and
the greatest of these is love.

~1 Corinthians 13:13

March 18

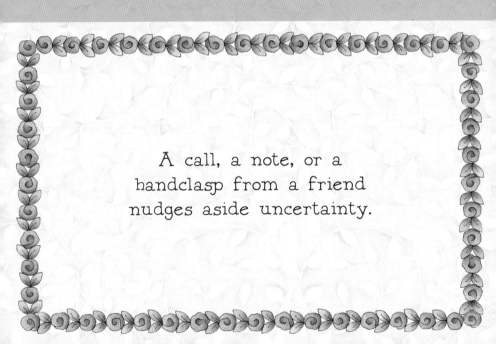

A call, a note, or a
handclasp from a friend
nudges aside uncertainty.

Till your soul, cultivate
blessings, grow joy.

March 19

Does everyone have an angel?
I believe they do.

October 28

Greater is he that is in you
than he that is in the world.

March 20

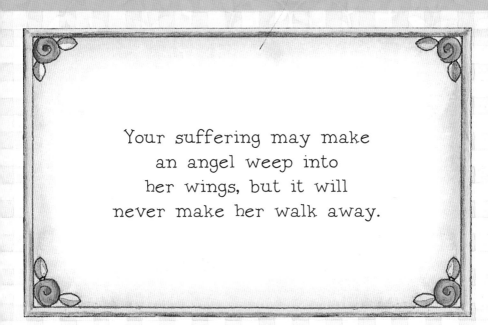

Your suffering may make
an angel weep into
her wings, but it will
never make her walk away.

Angels are all
around us, as far
as the heart can see.

March 21

Sadness is merely the absence of angels.

October 26

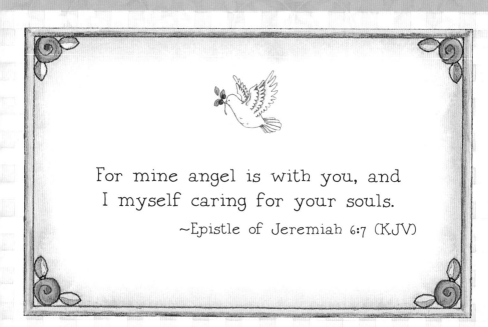

For mine angel is with you, and
I myself caring for your souls.

~Epistle of Jeremiah 6:7 (KJV)

March 22

There is no need to cry out
for your angels, for they
will come when your
heart calls for them.

October 25

If it is not of God,
it is not real.

March 23

Angels inhabit the
architecture of a
blessed body.

Want to grow spiritually?
Feed your spirit.

See rainbows in the rain
And sunbeams among the clouds,
And you will see as angels do.

October 23

Angels see
things from a
different angle.

March 25

You often find
an angel
in the smile
of a child.

Angels and ministers
of grace defend us!
~William Shakespeare

March 26

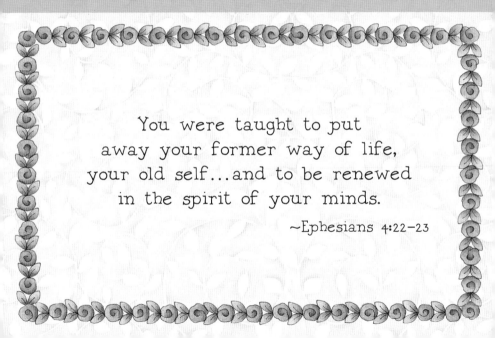

You were taught to put
away your former way of life,
your old self...and to be renewed
in the spirit of your minds.

~Ephesians 4:22–23

Ask yourself
each day,
"What is my
divine assignment?"

Wrap yourself in
your angel's wings
and be at peace.

October 20

Angels are the doctors
of our souls—they are
available twenty-four hours
a day, seven days a week,
work free of charge,
and make house calls!

Angels surround our lives
with love and protection.
Know that they are among
us to ease our burdens, shield
us from evil, lighten our hearts,
and guide us along our journeys.

October 19

The presence of angels is a
billboard that says, "You Matter!"

March 29

With my angel,
I am never alone.

Thus says the Lord:
"Stand at the crossroads,
and look, and ask for the
ancient paths, where the good
way lies; and walk in it, and
find rest for your souls."

~Jeremiah 6:16

March 30

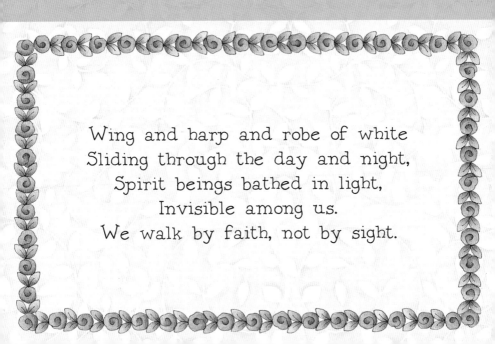

Wing and harp and robe of white
Sliding through the day and night,
Spirit beings bathed in light,
Invisible among us.
We walk by faith, not by sight.

October 17

To speak to angels,
all we need
is the intention.

March 31

There isn't a valley
so low that an
angel can't carry
you through it.

October 16

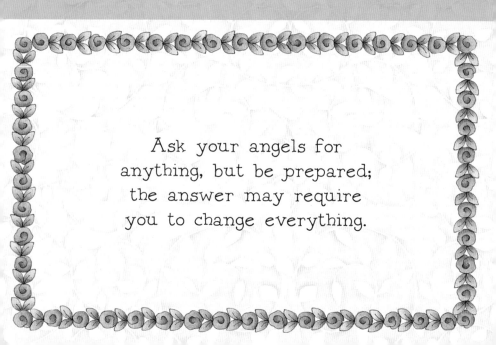

Ask your angels for
anything, but be prepared;
the answer may require
you to change everything.

There is one glory of the sun,
And another glory of the moon,
And another glory of the stars;
Indeed, star differs from star in glory.

~1 Corinthians 15:41

October 15

Live on earth
as you would
in heaven.

Why does the night sky sparkle? Each star is a jewel carried by an angel.

October 14

To all God's beloved...
who are called to be saints:
Grace and peace to you
from God our Father and
the Lord Jesus Christ.

~Romans 1:7

April 3

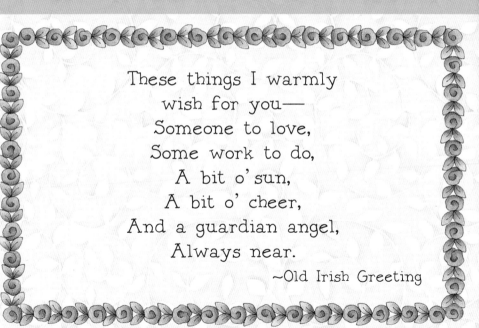

These things I warmly
wish for you—
Someone to love,
Some work to do,
A bit o' sun,
A bit o' cheer,
And a guardian angel,
Always near.

~Old Irish Greeting

Life seems to run wild,
but God holds the reins
and angels tend the harness.

April 4

For you who revere
my name the sun of
righteousness shall rise,
with healing in its wings.

~Malachi 4:2

October 12

To believe in an angel is to acknowledge that life is more than what we see. It is faith in action. It is a step toward seeing reality.

April 5

Bless our little ones today;
Bid your angels close to stay.
Protect them, Lord, as all the while
We see you in each sweet smile.

October 11

Footstep by footstep, your way is guarded.

Who's to say a
smile or a gentle
outstretched hand
from a stranger is
not an act of angels
in disguise?

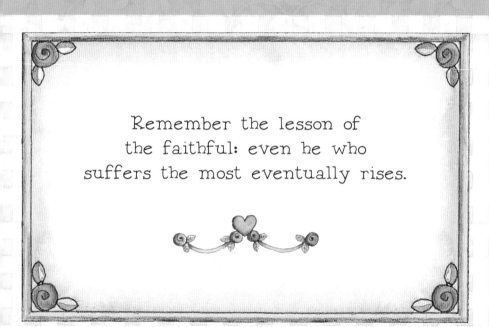

Remember the lesson of
the faithful: even he who
suffers the most eventually rises.

April 7

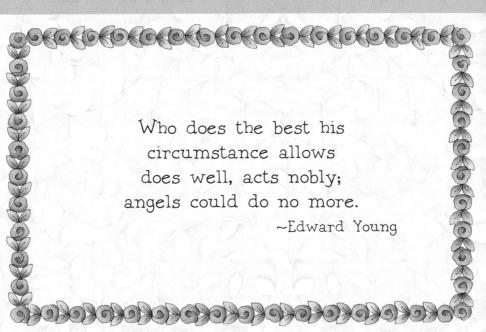

Who does the best his
circumstance allows
does well, acts nobly;
angels could do no more.

~Edward Young

October 9

Relish the life that
you have, for it is
the one God gave
you to embrace.

April 8

White winged angels
meet the child
On the vestibule of life.

~E. Oakes Smith

October 8

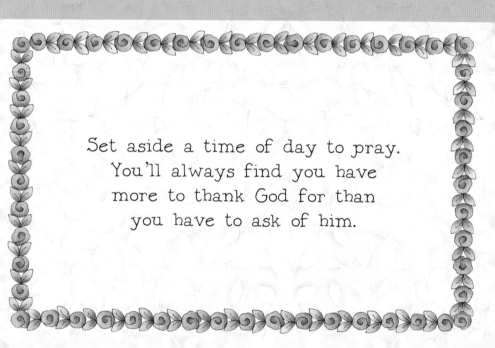

Set aside a time of day to pray.
You'll always find you have
more to thank God for than
you have to ask of him.

April 9

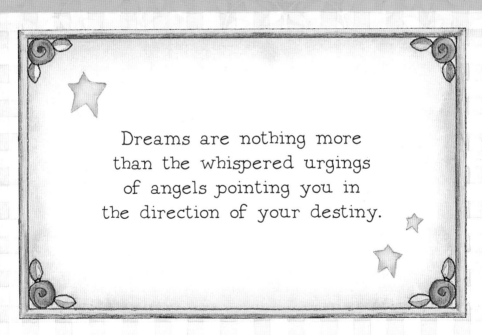

Dreams are nothing more
than the whispered urgings
of angels pointing you in
the direction of your destiny.

October 7

Angels fly above so
they can watch over us.

April 10

Beloved, let us love one another,
because love is from God; everyone who
loves is born of God and knows God.

~1 John 4:7

Relinquish the struggle.
Simply ask yourself,
"Is it divine?"

Angels exist in our
lives every day, but unless
we remember how to listen,
we are never aware
of their presence.

October 5

Sing praise!

Lord, help me make my heart a place where angels feel welcome.

Wherever on earth a light shines into a dark place, there will an angel be—shining hope into despair, love into hate, and tolerance into ignorance.

October 4

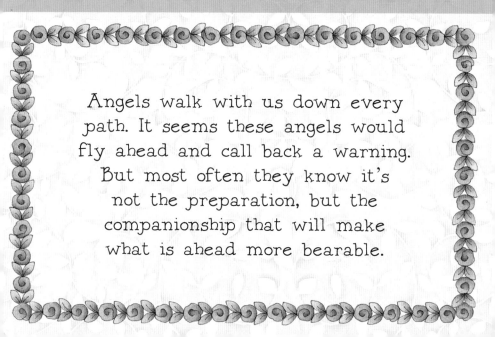

Angels walk with us down every path. It seems these angels would fly ahead and call back a warning. But most often they know it's not the preparation, but the companionship that will make what is ahead more bearable.

Wherever we are, if we open
our eyes to truly see, we will
find the wonder of God's handiwork.

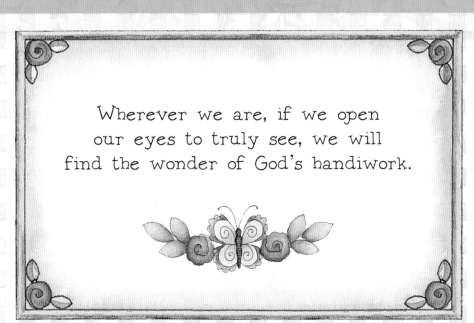

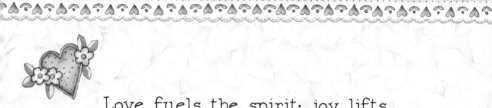

Love fuels the spirit; joy lifts
our hearts; hopes and dreams
float on angels' wings.

April 14

Songbirds are angels God sends to
herald each bright and blessed new day.

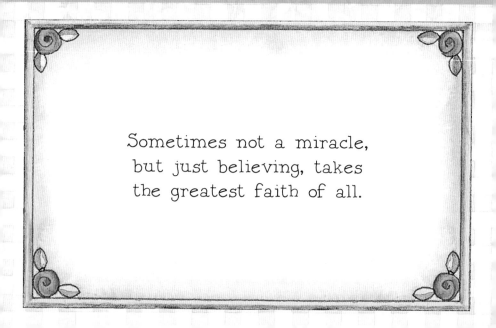

Sometimes not a miracle,
but just believing, takes
the greatest faith of all.

April 15

Where love is concerned,
an angel will do whatever
it takes to get the job done.

October 1

Let your heart
and mind be
lifted up on
the wings of angels.

Sing praise!

When a child is born, a multitude
of angels sing out in joy for the new
life that is about to bless the earth.

September 30

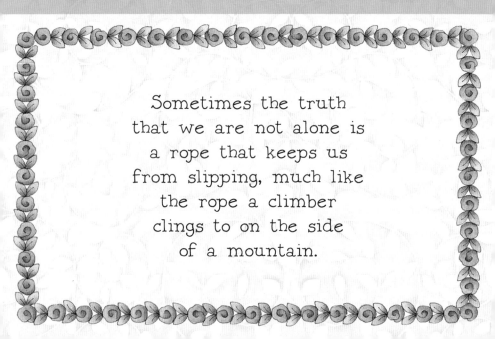

Sometimes the truth
that we are not alone is
a rope that keeps us
from slipping, much like
the rope a climber
clings to on the side
of a mountain.

April 17

Angels fill our days
With love and light.
And watch over us
As we sleep at night.

September 29

Let each of you look
not to your own
interests, but to the
interests of others.

~Philippians 2:4

April 18

Angels look for the best in us,
and they nourish that place.
They see who God has created us to be,
and they push that vision into reality.

Let me walk beside you;
I won't ask you to support me.
I only want to know
That I am not alone.

April 19

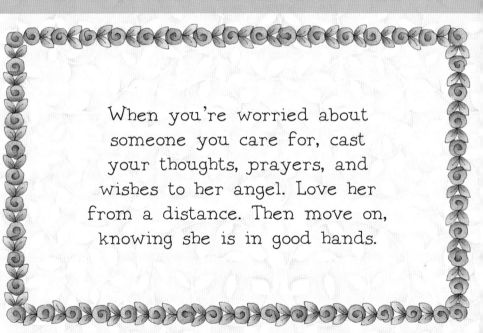

When you're worried about someone you care for, cast your thoughts, prayers, and wishes to her angel. Love her from a distance. Then move on, knowing she is in good hands.

September 27

Life is full of moments
that only you and
your angel share.

Whenever a baby giggles,
an angel is smiling too.

September 26

Each of us has at least
one angel in our life.
Find yours and give thanks.

April 21

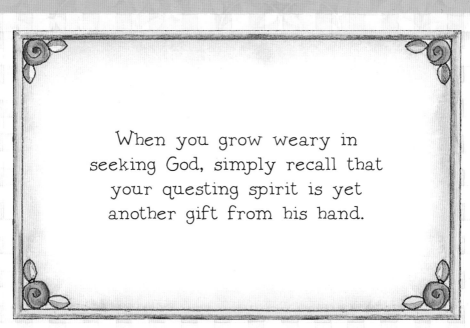

When you grow weary in seeking God, simply recall that your questing spirit is yet another gift from his hand.

September 25

Sing praise!

Why do the angels sing?
Because they are instruments of God.

April 22

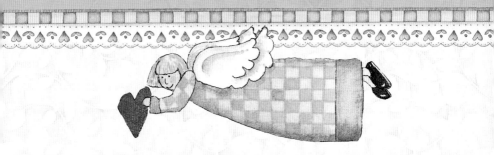

It's a comforting thought to know
that angels work and move among us
to make the most of the love we have.

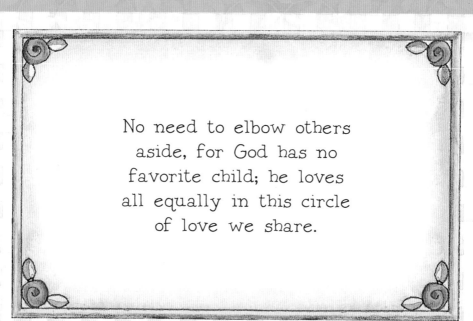

No need to elbow others
aside, for God has no
favorite child; he loves
all equally in this circle
of love we share.

April 23

When you feel lost, pause and
look closely around you.
Somewhere, somehow, an angel
will be waiting to guide you home.

September 23

And when we cried
to the Lord, he heard our
voice, and sent an angel.

~Numbers 20:16

April 24

Though the answers
always come from God,
our questions about
life's trials must first
be directed to ourselves.

September 22

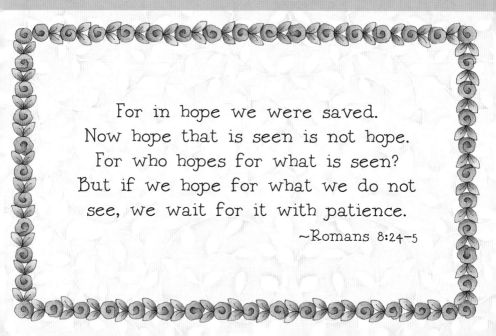

For in hope we were saved.
Now hope that is seen is not hope.
For who hopes for what is seen?
But if we hope for what we do not
see, we wait for it with patience.

~Romans 8:24-5

Faith converses with the angels,
and antedates the hymns of glory.

~Jeremy Taylor

September 21

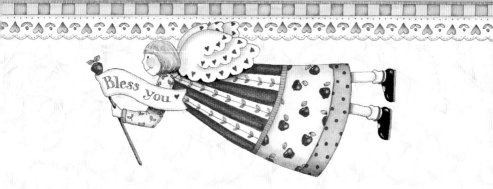

Angel, guide my heart and hands
to reach beyond myself this day.

April 26

When you feel burdened by haunting
memories, you can always choose
to lift your eyes and shift your focus.

And when you turn to the right or when you turn to the left, your ears shall hear a word behind you, saying, "This is the way; walk in it."

~Isaiah 30:21

April 27

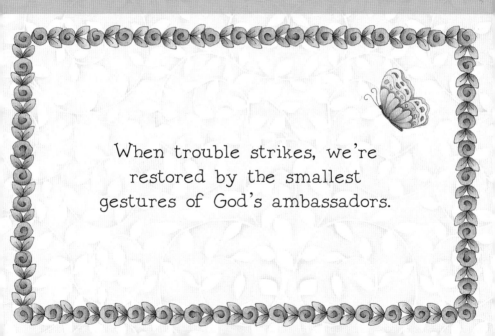

When trouble strikes, we're restored by the smallest gestures of God's ambassadors.

September 19

Angels provide a
resting place for
weary souls on their
way to heaven.

When the rain falls
and the wind blows,
wrap yourself in your
angel's perfect love.

September 18

Angels are messengers
from a place far beyond
our own. We do well
when we listen.

April 29

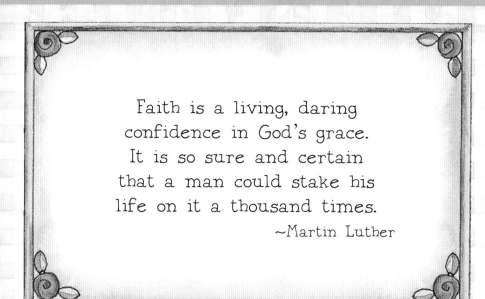

Faith is a living, daring
confidence in God's grace.
It is so sure and certain
that a man could stake his
life on it a thousand times.
~Martin Luther

September 17

Looking for the Lord?
Simply follow the angels.

April 30

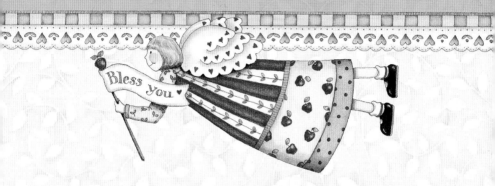

Bless you ♥

Angels bring a heavenly
dimension to everyday life.

September 16

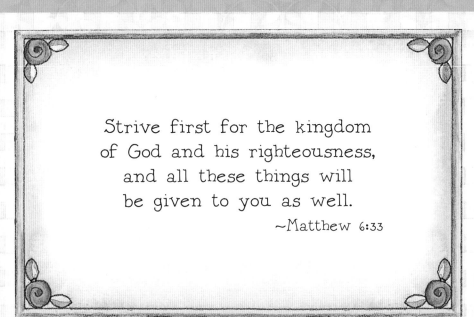

Strive first for the kingdom
of God and his righteousness,
and all these things will
be given to you as well.

~Matthew 6:33

May 1

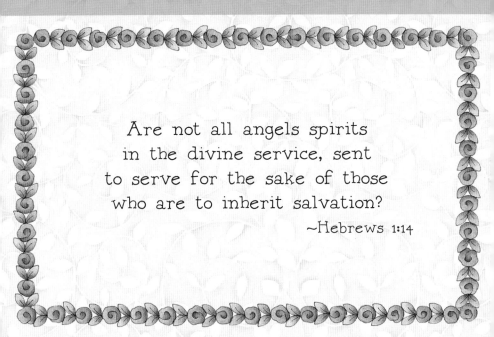

Are not all angels spirits
in the divine service, sent
to serve for the sake of those
who are to inherit salvation?

~Hebrews 1:14

Strong yet gentle, angels
are spiritual warriors
of peace, joy, and love.

May 2

Every visible thing
in this world is put in
the charge of an angel.

~Saint Augustine

September 14

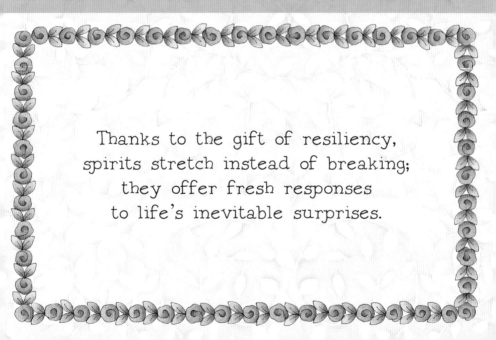

Thanks to the gift of resiliency,
spirits stretch instead of breaking;
they offer fresh responses
to life's inevitable surprises.

May 3

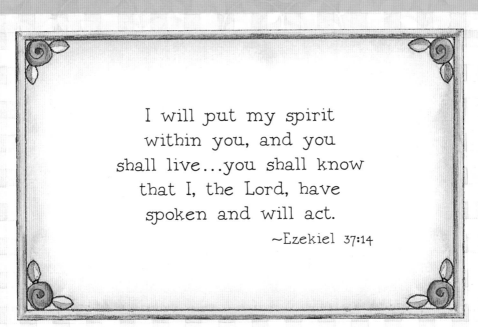

I will put my spirit
within you, and you
shall live...you shall know
that I, the Lord, have
spoken and will act.

~Ezekiel 37:14

September 13

If we are to believe in angels,
we must first believe that we can fly.

May 4

I'd like to see
an angel dance.
I'd like to dance along.

His spirit will guide us;
the angels will guard us.

May 5

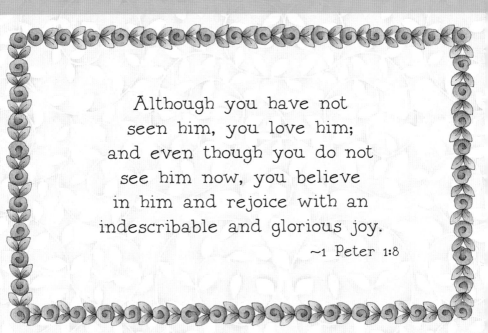

Although you have not
seen him, you love him;
and even though you do not
see him now, you believe
in him and rejoice with an
indescribable and glorious joy.

~1 Peter 1:8

September 11

The greatest gift
we can give
ourselves is God.

May 6

Tend your relationship
with God as though
it is a garden, and
you will see it bloom.

September 10

Today, I open my eyes
to see who is looking
with a plea for help.

May 7

Always listen for an
angel's voice, and you'll
speak more gently yourself.

September 9

Exercise your heart—
be an angel!

May 8

Each step I take down the path angels trod
Is another step closer to God.

You cannot grant
forgiveness without
giving love.

May 9

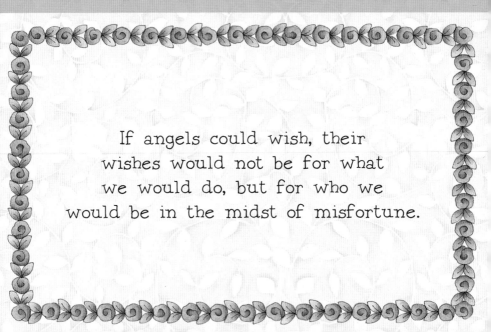

If angels could wish, their wishes would not be for what we would do, but for who we would be in the midst of misfortune.

September 7

Sing praise!

Sing on high,
for the chorus
of angels
is listening.

Like sunlight in the mind, cheerfulness lasts far longer than the lightning-like burst of amusement that glitters for only a split second.

September 6

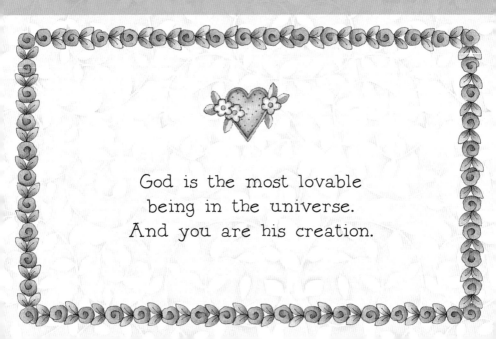

God is the most lovable
being in the universe.
And you are his creation.

Like an eagle gracefully
soaring, wings outstretched,
feel the updraft of air and
rest awhile, trusting that God
is the wind beneath your wings.

September 5

Our wounds may
not be the work
of God, but he
helps heal them.

May 12

It's said that angels come from heaven, but I have met a fair share of them right here on earth.

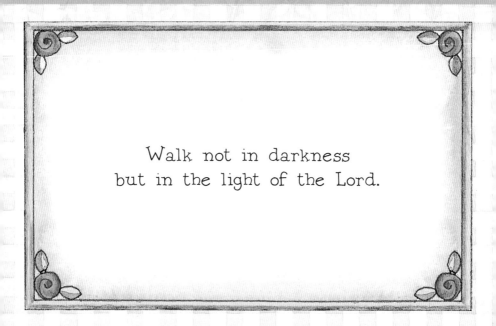

Walk not in darkness
but in the light of the Lord.

May 13

It's not your imagination.
Sometimes a "coincidence"
comes with a lot of angelic effort.

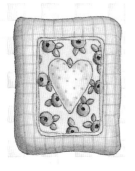

Don't give up. Even the halo of an angel needs a little elbow grease to shine.

May 14

Listen for your angels,
and they'll sing you a
tune—but only when
you listen closely.

When we are heavy
with sorrow we must look
to our angels to help us fly.

May 15

God is faithful, and he will not let
you be tested beyond your strength,
but with the testing he will also
provide the way out so that
you may be able to endure it.

~1 Corinthians 10:13

September 1

They are to do good, to be rich in good works, generous, and ready to share.

~1 Timothy 6:18

May 16

Angels can fly because they
take themselves lightly.

~G.K. Chesterton

They also serve who
only stand and wait.

~John Milton

May 17

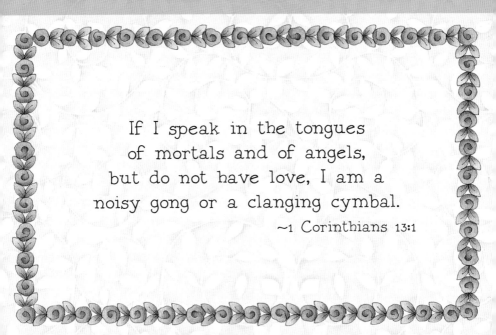

If I speak in the tongues
of mortals and of angels,
but do not have love, I am a
noisy gong or a clanging cymbal.

~1 Corinthians 13:1

Relinquish your
burdens to
your angels.

May 18

If angels wear colors,
they are surely
every nuance of
a rainbow.

There are moments during
the day that are undeniably
touched by angels.

May 19

Jesus said, "Take care that you do not despise one of these little ones; for, I tell you, in heaven their angels continually see the face of my father in heaven."

~Matthew 18:10

August 28

The unlikeliest
of people harbor
halos beneath
their hats.

May 20

As long as
angels are all
around us, God
is everywhere.

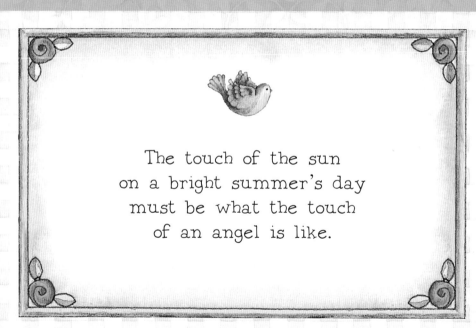

The touch of the sun
on a bright summer's day
must be what the touch
of an angel is like.

May 21

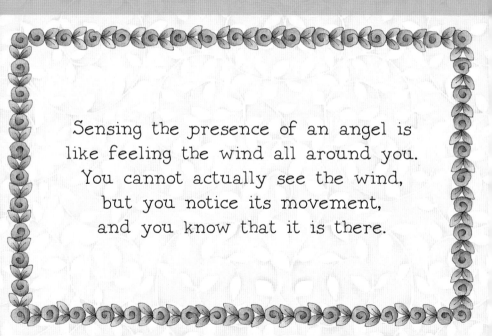

Sensing the presence of an angel is
like feeling the wind all around you.
You cannot actually see the wind,
but you notice its movement,
and you know that it is there.

August 26

Angels are our
direct link to heaven.

May 22

Greet each new day
with new hope.
Even broken halos
can be repaired.

August 25

The strength of an angel
is her purity. Truth be
known, this is the
strength of all of us.

May 23

In your deepest distress
you are often covered
by angels' wings on every side.

August 24

The spirit of the Lord God...
has sent me to bring good news...
to proclaim the year of the Lord's favor.

~Isaiah 61:1-2

May 24

The flight of angels
is God's word, rising.

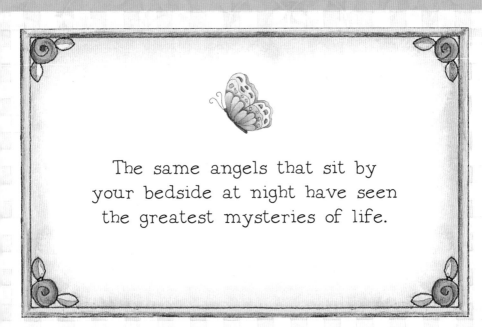

The same angels that sit by
your bedside at night have seen
the greatest mysteries of life.

May 25

Blessed are the peacemakers,
for they will be called
children of God.

~Matthew 5:9

May you be blessed
to know God's abiding
presence at work today!

May 26

Live where angels dwell.

August 21

Angels give of themselves
fully, for they have
seen the face of love.

May 27

If you want to hear the
sound of an angel's wings,
listen to your own heartbeat.

August 20

God lifts us up. Angels help us fly.

May 28

To do a good deed, one does not need a halo—only the will to do good.

August 19

The ignorant say they will
believe in angels only when
they see them. The wise
understand they will see angels
only when they believe in them.

To rise up like an angel,
you must first
spread your wings.

August 18

Angels beside me,
lead me and guide me.

May 30

We stand tallest
after we've knelt
before the Lord.

August 17

The days, the hours,
the minutes of our
lives are guarded and
observed by heaven.

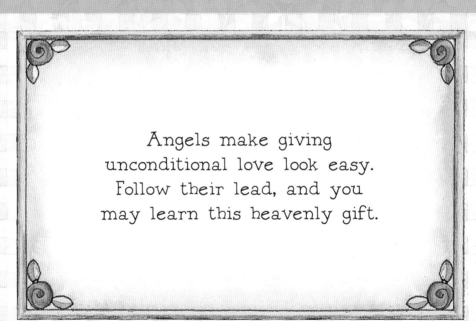

Angels make giving
unconditional love look easy.
Follow their lead, and you
may learn this heavenly gift.

August 16

Angels' wings gain
strength with our prayers.

June 1

Bless you ♥

A day without prayer is as dark as night.

Angels often speak to
us in dreams, when the
intellect is asleep and the
intuition is tuned in to the
frequencies of the spirit.

June 2

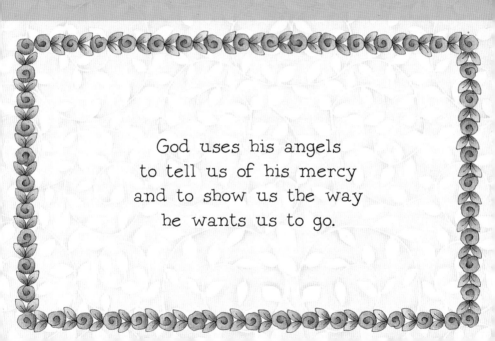

God uses his angels
to tell us of his mercy
and to show us the way
he wants us to go.

August 14

Many an arrow
thrown by love
is followed by
an angel's breath
of promise.

Angels are observers
who walk the pace of
a person who has all
the time in the world.

August 13

May you always walk
with the morning star
to guide you, the summer
sun on your back, and
an angel by your side.

June 4

God gives you millions of paths.
Trust, then, that the heart he gave
you will choose the right one.

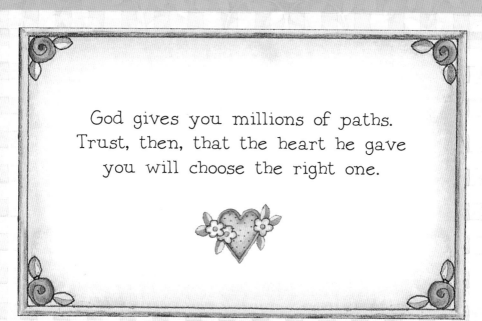

Love, that power that makes
a difference, covers the
lives of those it touches.

June 5

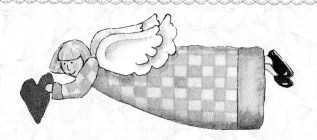

So long as we can count on God,
we can count our blessings.

Sweet souls around us watch us still,
Press nearer to our side;
Into our thoughts, into our prayers,
With gentle helpings glide.

~Harriet Beecher Stowe

June 6

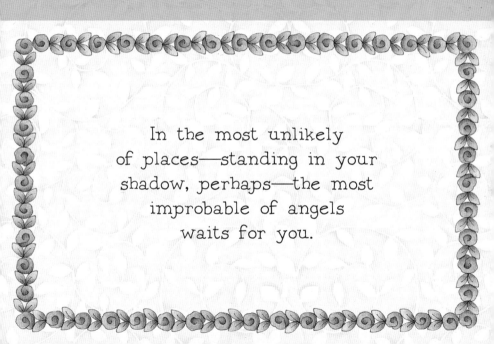

In the most unlikely
of places—standing in your
shadow, perhaps—the most
improbable of angels
waits for you.

If rain is an
angel's tears,
then a star is
her heart aglow.

We feel lost
only when we
have lost the
way to God.

August 9

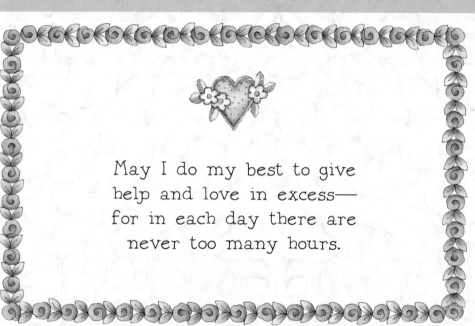

May I do my best to give
help and love in excess—
for in each day there are
never too many hours.

June 8

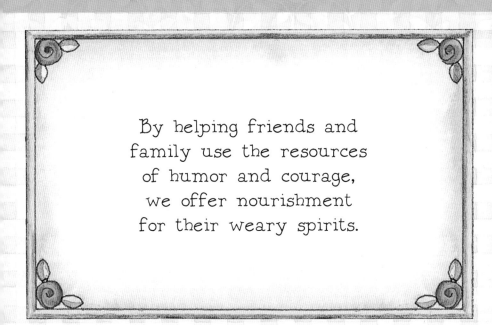

By helping friends and
family use the resources
of humor and courage,
we offer nourishment
for their weary spirits.

August 8

Fly on, sweet spirit,
and make straight and safe
the path I must walk today.

June 9

To believe in angels is to celebrate a reality you cannot see and to respect a realm for which you are not yet ready.

For I am convinced that neither death,
nor life, nor angels, nor rulers,
nor things present, nor things to come,
nor powers, nor height, nor depth,
nor anything else in all creation, will
be able to separate us from the love
of God in Christ Jesus our Lord.

~Romans 8:38–39

Let an angel into your life
and joy and comfort will
follow you wherever you go.

If you want to feel
happy, look inward.
If you want to feel
blessed, look skyward.

June 11

There is no stronger bond
than the one we share
with our father in heaven.

August 5

Thank goodness for angels and children; they have so much in common. Both are pure in heart and have boundless ability to love.

June 12

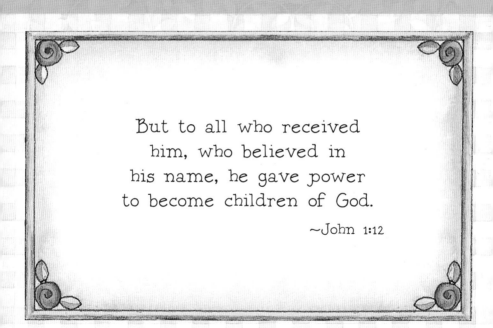

But to all who received
him, who believed in
his name, he gave power
to become children of God.

~John 1:12

August 4

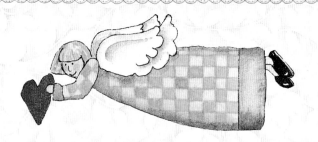

Thank you for my
life's precious gifts, Lord.

June 13

Sing praise!

Alone is impossible
in a world inhabited by angels.

August 3

Sometimes in the hazy morning between "waking up" and "not yet," take the time to listen to your soul. You'll find you can hear your angels telling you to be ready for the day. It's the best wake-up call there is.

June 14

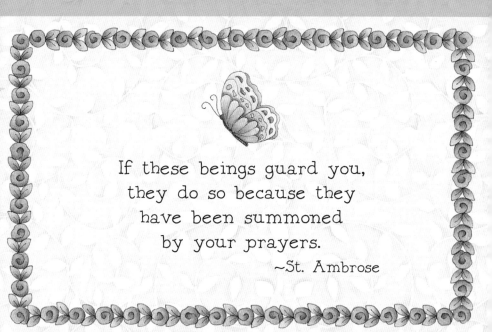

If these beings guard you,
they do so because they
have been summoned
by your prayers.

~St. Ambrose

August 2

May you know the
love of the angels,
deep as the ocean,
steadfast as the stars.

June 15

The higher power
is the highest power.

August 1

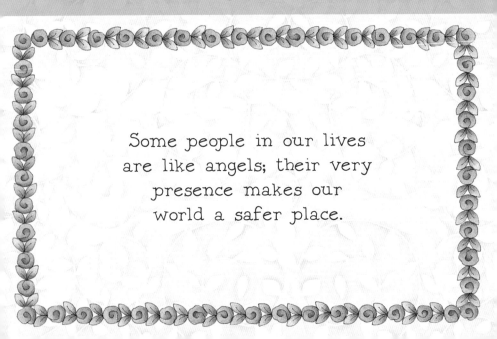

Some people in our lives
are like angels; their very
presence makes our
world a safer place.

Always help to heal the broken
wings of others—you never
know who might be an angel.

July 31

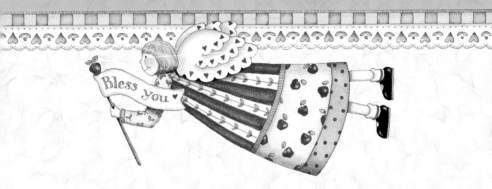

Thanks for standing by me, angel,
even when I am at my least lovable.

June 17

Friends are simply
angels without wings.

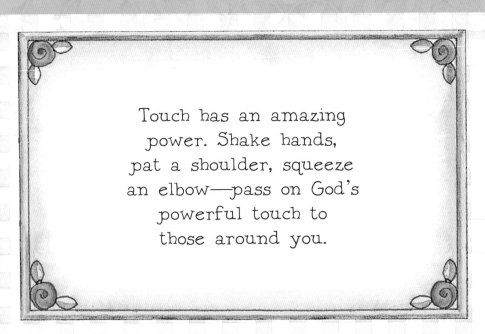

Touch has an amazing
power. Shake hands,
pat a shoulder, squeeze
an elbow—pass on God's
powerful touch to
those around you.

June 18

The fruit of the spirit is
love, joy, peace, patience,
kindness, generosity, faithfulness,
gentleness, and self-control.

~Galatians 5:22-23

July 29

True friends are like
angels among us.

June 19

Give voice to
God's word—
speak kindly.

Tools for building peace
include a kind heart,
sturdy hands, and faith
in each rebuilt bridge.

June 20

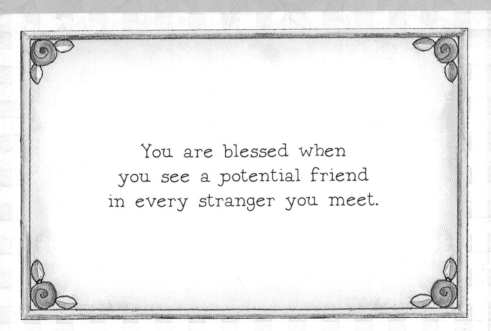

You are blessed when
you see a potential friend
in every stranger you meet.

July 27

Angels are the
power of goodness.
They lend their
strength to those
who do good.

June 21

Trust your
intuition.
It's the voice
of your angel.

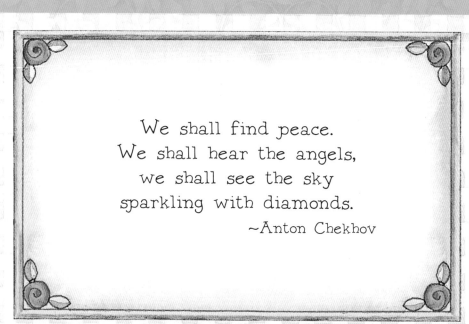

We shall find peace.
We shall hear the angels,
we shall see the sky
sparkling with diamonds.

~Anton Chekhov

June 22

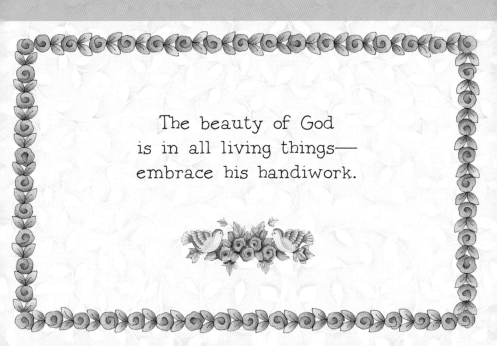

The beauty of God
is in all living things—
embrace his handiwork.

July 25

True friendship is
a knot that angel
hands have tied.

~Anonymous

June 23

Live wisely,
love wholly.

July 24

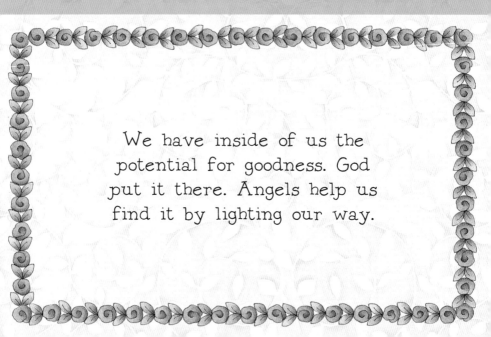

We have inside of us the potential for goodness. God put it there. Angels help us find it by lighting our way.

June 24

Blessed are the pure in
heart, for they will see God.

~Matthew 5:8

July 23

We do ourselves the most good when we are doing something for others.

~Horace Mann

June 25

In those moments
when your spirit
is weary, be still
and feel God's
presence overflowing.

Bungling, blundering, feeling
so alone, we struggle through
some days only to find when
the fog has lifted we are just
where we should be—in the
company of angels.

June 26

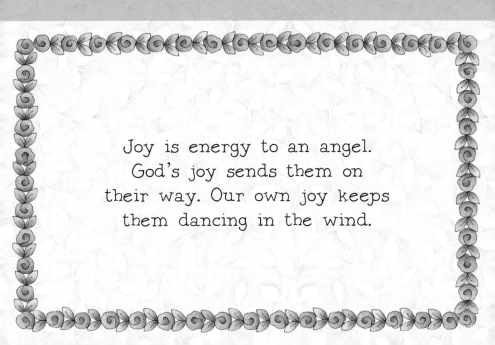

Joy is energy to an angel.
God's joy sends them on
their way. Our own joy keeps
them dancing in the wind.

July 21

Trust your angels
to guide your steps.

Angels are the closest thing to heaven that we carry with us every day.

July 20

We can often learn to
recognize the sound of an
angel's voice when we listen
to the little urge to do the
right thing, to go the extra mile.

June 28

The guardian angel of
life sometimes flies so
high that man cannot see it;
but he always is looking
down upon us, and will
soon hover nearer to us.

~Jean Paul Richter

July 19

Angels sometimes come in choirs and sometimes they come alone, but they come most often when they aren't expected.

June 29

Your journey may be long, but
so long as you believe in angels,
you will never walk alone.

July 18

Were there no God,
we would be in this glorious
world with grateful hearts:
and no one to thank.

~Christina Rossetti

June 30

When someone we love
passes away from this
world, it can ease the
pain to realize we have
not lost a friend, but
have gained an angel.

July 17

We stand as tall as angels
when we kneel to
help a friend.

July 1

Faith in mankind begins
with faith in oneself.

What a grand thing, to be loved!
What a grander thing still, to love!

~Victor Hugo

July 2

When I feel my efforts at
goodness are disappearing, I look
for the small things from kith
and kin, neighbor and stranger,
that suggest I am succeeding.

Angels, contented with their fame in
Heaven, seek not the praise of men.

~John Milton

July 3

When seeking help,
I must be willing
to trust those who
offer—and the God
who sends them.

July 14

If you woo the company of the angels
in your waking hours, they will be
sure to come to you in your sleep.

~G. D. Prentice

July 4

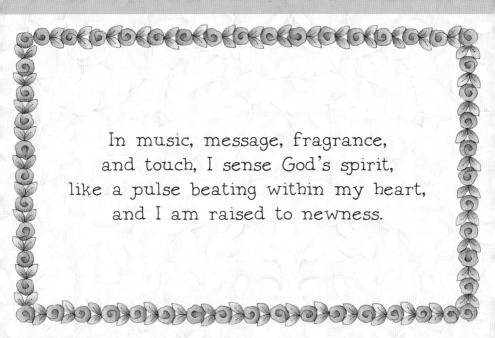

In music, message, fragrance,
and touch, I sense God's spirit,
like a pulse beating within my heart,
and I am raised to newness.

Angels come to us
in many forms.
Be open to
receive them.

July 5

When I admire your creation, Lord, I can't stay silent. I must shout with jubilation!

July 12

Love is patient; love is kind;
love is not envious or boastful
or arrogant or rude.

~1 Corinthians 13:4-5

July 6

What know we of the Blest above
But that they sing,
And that they love?

~William Wordsworth

Angels are counselors sent from God.

July 7

May you have sunshine and
moon song and angels as
your constant companions.

Angels must see us much differently than we see ourselves. We so often concentrate on our weaknesses, our faults. But angels see us from the inside out because they see us through the love of God.

July 8

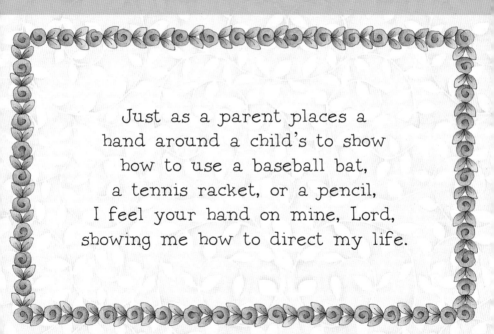

Just as a parent places a
hand around a child's to show
how to use a baseball bat,
a tennis racket, or a pencil,
I feel your hand on mine, Lord,
showing me how to direct my life.

July 9

Angels descending,
bringing from above
Echoes of mercy,
whispers of love.

~Fanny J. Crosby